Lori,

Thank you for your
Support and our growth
together in Christ

Love
Shirley Fitzgerald Oliver
1/96 ☺!

Oh Lord!
Have Mercy

By Shirley A. Fitzgerald

Fairway Press
Lima, Ohio

OH LORD! HAVE MERCY

FIRST EDITION
Copyright © 1991 by
Shirley Oliver

7748 / ISBN 1-55673-249-X   PRINTED IN U.S.A.

Who would have thought the little girl who once chased butterflies and picked flowers in a grave-yard, would grow up one day to write a book. Oh Lord! Have Mercy.

Hear me when I call, O God of my righteousness: thou hast enlarged me when I was in distress: have mercy upon me, and hear my prayer. Psalms 4:1

Table of Contents

Chapter

Chapter 1
Hear My Cry Oh Lord

*In my distress I cried into the LORD, and he heard
me.* (Psalms 120:1)

The inspiration for this book came from experiences in
which I had to ask God to have mercy on me. Through trials
and tribulations, grief and despair, headaches, heartaches, and
in times of trouble and sickness, I had to ask God to have mercy
on me and he heard my cry and solved my problems.

The problems we experience in life are not ours alone to
bear. God has given us specific instructions as to what to do
with our problems and burdens. Often times, we choose to
handle our problems ourselves within our own strength. We
wrestle with them until they beat us into the ground. It is not
until we are too tired to fight and become totally whipped by
our problems, when we turn to God and cry out Oh Lord!
Have Mercy.

Sometimes in life we take God's goodness and mercy for
granted. We allow self to direct our thoughts and actions.

Self gets us in trouble all the time. Self causes us to have
self doubt, causing us self defeat, and self destruction. Self
doubt comes when we do not exercise our faith and believe
that God has created us in his image, in his likeness, and into
someone beautiful, capable of achieving all things.

Self defeat causes us to work against our own God given
talents and potentialities. We constantly find reasons why we
can't achieve. We make excuses of being too fat, skinny,
young, old, or too short, tall, ugly, poor, or too dumb. You
name it, we can come up with a bonafide reason why we can't
achieve. Frankly, I believe we are just too AFRAID to allow
God to operate in our lives through the Holy Spirit. "God has
not given us the spirit of fear; but of power, and of love, and

7

of a sound mind.'' (2 Timothy 7:1) Rather than putting our trust in God we often times put our confidence in our spouses, children, friends, or other professionals. When we learn to put our trust in God, we will realize we have victory in him.

We must be aware of forces that are not of God which leads us toward self destruction. Self destruction can be readily seen in the habitual drug and alcohol user. Self destruction can also be hidden in over-indulging in food, work, men or women. Over-indulgence in any of the above, can cause health problems as well as problems in our homes, schools, work environment or social settings.

Oh Lord! Have Mercy should be our constant cry. When our tender hearts are broken, we can ask God to have mercy and he will fix it. When we are disappointed and discouraged along our life Journey, we can ask the Lord to have mercy. All of us have experienced the pain of disappointment by having our hearts broken by someone we trusted. After our deep hurt, we asked God to have mercy, he moved into our hearts to wash away the pain, and the tears began to fall. Tears have a cleansing power, they allow the heart to be clean, thereby easing the pain.

God Knows Best

Our Father knows what's best for us,
so why should we complain?
We always want the sunshine,
but he knows there must be rain.

We love the sound of laughter
and the merriment of cheer.
But our hearts will lose
their tenderness if we never
shed a tear.

Our Father tests us often with
suffering and sorrow.
He tests us not to punish us,
but to help us tomorrow.

For going on you need these things
to withstand the storm.
For the straight cut of the chisel
gives the marble grace and form.

He never hurts us needlessly
and He never wants our pain.
For every loss He sends us
is followed by rich gain.

And when we count the blessings
that God has so freely sent,
we will find no cause for
murmuring, and no time for
lament.

For our Father loves His children.
And to Him all things are plain.
He never sends us a pleasure,
when the soul's deep need is pain.

So when we are troubled,
and when everything goes wrong.
It is just God working,
to make our Spirit strong.

Yvonne Audrey
(1940-1989)

The above poem was written by my cousin Yvonne Audrey the night before she went home to live with God. Yvonne left a message to encourage all of us to believe and trust in God. The words which poured from her soul can be used as tools to lift the Spirits of others.

God is a good God, he hears us when we call and loves us very much. He wants only what is best for us. He only asks that we believe in him, trust him and never doubt. He has promised to work things out and answer when we call.

Chapter 2
In Times of Trouble

The LORD also will be a refuge for the oppressed,
a refuge in times of trouble. (Psalms 9:9)

All of us at one time or another have experienced trouble. Trouble is all around us, in our homes, in our schools and on our jobs. Credit cards, extended credit and liberties to buy now and pay later, get us into financial trouble. Other people give us trouble, our spouses, children, relatives and associates. We also experience trouble in the physical sense with our hearts, minds, backs, and even trouble with our feet. There is no getting around trouble. Trouble is any unfortunate distressing situation or circumstance which causes us sorrow, misery or pain.

We often hear "Nobody knows the trouble I've seen" implying the trouble they have experienced was so unbearable that no one would believe they had such trouble. Some of us don't know when we are in it, until we can't get out of it. Whatever you call it, all of us have had it. None of us want it, but we can't seem to live without it. Trouble is nothing new.

The Word of God tells us we will have trouble. We are reminded of the trouble experienced by Job, a perfect and an upright man who feared God and hated evil. Job was tried and tested by Satan to see if he would curse God. Job lost all of his children and animals and was inflicted with sickness. But rather than curse God, Job worshipped God and said, "Naked came I out of my mother's womb, and naked shall I return thither: The LORD gave, and the LORD hath taken away; blessed be the name of the LORD." (Job 1:20-21)

When Job pondered over his situation, he said "I was not in safety, neither had I rest, neither was I quiet; yet trouble came." (Job 3:26) "Although affliction cometh not forth the dust, neither doth trouble spring out of the ground; Yet man

11

is born into trouble, as the sparks fly upward." (Job 5:6-7) "Man that is born of a woman is of few days, and full of trouble." (Job 14:1)

When we are in trouble we have a hope even unto death. "We are troubled on every side, yet not distressed; we are perplexed, but not in despair." (1 Corinthians 4:8-9) Whatever trouble we have, there is someone worse off than us.

My cousin Charles experienced trouble. One Sunday night he was stabbed and no one was able to locate his immediate family, so they called me. I had just gotten home from visiting my Aunt Rose, who had recently suffered a stroke. Aunt Rose helped raise me when I was younger and was in her seventies. My visit with her in the hospital had been a pleasant but tiring one. My past week had been busy and hectic and I looked forward to relaxing when I got home. I had just walked through the door when the telephone rang. It was Charles's neighbor. He said, "Charles has been stabbed. It looks pretty bad, I don't think he is going to make it." In my silence, all I could say was "Oh Lord! Have Mercy."

I managed to locate one of his brothers. However, somehow I knew he did not want to hear bad news that night. Therefore, I was left to find out the details. I didn't know Charles that well, but he had worked for us from time to time. Often Charles would work for us awhile and then we would not see or hear from him until his money ran out. Once I told him he did a good job, but we worked every week, five days a week. He would just smile and say "Okay, Shirley." He was always pleasant and respectable around me. I talked briefly with him a few times, but never criticized him for the type of life he lived. However, at this point I realized Charles was in trouble at death's door and needed someone who cared.

I called the rescue squad to find out what hospital they had taken him. I tried to find someone to go with me to the hospital but was unable to locate anyone. I had to go alone. As I drove to the hospital, I began to reflect on the trials and tribulations Charles had experienced. He was divorced but wanted to get back with his wife. He had tried to locate her but was unable to find her because she had moved away. He had difficulties holding a steady job because he had a serious drinking problem and often associated with people not in his best interest.

As I drove in the dark, I regretted I had not been able to reach his inner soul to help turn his life around. Somehow I felt as if I was mentally communicating with him, telling him that even though he was in the valley of the shadow of death, he still had a chance to turn his life over to God and turn his life around. I felt this had to be the turning point for Charles. He was at a point in which I felt he had no choice but to change his life and turn it over to God.

After reaching the hospital, I realized he had been taken to the shock trauma department. The shock trauma section was in the back of the hospital and I had to grope around in the dark to find the entrance. Finally, I saw a path which led to the door of the shock trauma section. A helicopter had just landed and a police officer let me in.

Once inside, I had a difficult time finding the room number the rescue squad had given me. I went up and down the hall looking for the room number. I saw a minister walking down the hall and I asked him for help. He looked at me and asked who was I looking for. I gave him Charles' name. He then told me to wait there, he would be right back. He went in a room directly across from us and came back with a man in a white lab coat. The man started asking me quesitons about Charles. I answered them. First he asked me what relationship I was to him. Then he asked if he had any other relatives. He wanted to know where he lived, and how old he was. Then it suddenly dawned on me, he had asked all the questions in the past tense. I asked him why was he asking the questions in a past tense. He informed me Charles had died 30 minutes ago.

The LORD is good and his mercies ENDURETH for ever. We can not stand in judgement of the life Charles lived, because according to the Word of God, ''we all have sinned and come short of the Glory of God.'' (Romans 3:23)

Charles' life was filled with trials, tribulations and trouble. Charles, like many of us at one time or another, had troubles he felt he could not face alone. It is no secret that Charles tried to hide his trouble by drinking. Some of us try various means to hide our troubles. Some of us use work, money, food, or drugs to escape from our troubles, which often times make matters worse.

Charles was basically a good-hearted person. When the U.S. Army called him for service, he served. He received medals, recognitions and a honorable discharge. When he worked, he was a good worker, taking great pride in his work. When he had something to share, he shared. When someone needed help, he helped when he could.

I had no tears of sorrow for Charles. Sure, I will miss him and think of him often. But I believe that Charles has gone to a better place, his troubles in this life are over. I believe he is at rest. I believe when Charles realized that he was in trouble, in the valley of the shadow of death, at the end of his rope, boxed-in, with no way out, taking all he could take, he had no choice but to let go and turn his life over to God. I believe the LORD heard him, answered him and delivered him out of his distress.

Charles' trouble in this life is over. The kind of trouble WE have, we can LIVE with. Whenever we are facing a problem we can rest assured someone somewhere has gone through the same thing we are facing and have made it. There is no new trouble. According to the Word of God, "the thing that hath been, it is that which shall be; and that which is done is that which shall be done; and there is no new thing under the sun." (Ecclesiastes 1:9) No new troubles.

When we feel that no one has had our problem, we need only to share it with someone close to find out we are not alone. Talking about your problem will help in solving it.

When we make the decision to change our situation, we need to seek advice from those in a position to help us. They can help us identify the underlying root of our problem by looking beyond the circumstances to find the real problem.

When we are having trouble paying the mortgage, providing food and clothing, our problem is insufficient income: we need a better paying job. When our sons or daughters are in trouble, our problem is misunderstanding: we need to seek counseling. When we are in financial trouble, our problem is over-spending: we need to start living within our budget. There is a solution to our problems and someone somewhere will help us.

Some people take great pride in solving other people's problems, it gives them a sense of satisfaction knowing that they have helped someone who was in trouble.

Many organizations and churches are waiting to help those in need, assisting with food, clothing and shelter. Social Services will provide counseling for family members and financial support may be just a phone call away.

Regardless of what kind of trouble we are facing now, there is someone who can and will help us. When we seek help we will find it. People have lost their jobs, homes and loved ones for generations hence. Parents have not been able to provide clothing, food or shelter for their families. People have disobeyed the law and children have gotten into all sorts of trouble before. Trouble should not come as a surprise to us.

We do, however, have a hope and a refuge in our LORD and Savior Jesus Christ. He has promised to be a refuge for the oppressed, and a refuge in times of trouble. (Psalms 9:9) God is our refuge and strength, a very present help in trouble. (Psalms 46:1) For in the time of trouble he shall hide us in his pavilion: (Psalms 27:5) and comfort us in all our tribulations so that we will be able to comfort those in their time of trouble. (2 Corinthians 1:4) He will provide pastors, lawyers, doctors, bankers and even strangers to help us get out of trouble if we seek help.

GOD IS OUR ANSWER IN TIMES OF TROUBLE: he is a loving, caring and compassionate God. He is a refuge in time of trouble. (Psalms 9:9) A very present help in trouble. (Psalms 46:1) He will shield, hide and protect us. (Psalms 27:5) He will bring peace, and tranquility and deliver us out of our distress.

We need only to believe and trust in him, tell him all about our troubles, read his Word, thank him for his hiding place and his promise to deliver us from our troubles.

Chapter 3
In Despair

. . . to all living there is hope. (Ecclesiastes 9:4)

Hopelessness, despondency, gloom and depression are leading causes that make us lose our faith, confidence, and courage when faced with a problem. Our minds become preoccupied with our circumstances, which seem too much to bear and we abandon hope.

We can not allow fear, worry, uncertainty, anxiety or any other sense of powerlessness deteriorate or destroy our spirit of hope. There is always hope, for without hope we would be lost. When the storms of life are raging and the rain seems like it will never stop, we can hope for a brighter tomorrow filled with sunshine and happiness. Without hope for a better tomorrow, we could easily give up.

Sometimes we want things in life right now. We become so keyed-up with our situation, we can't eat, sleep, work or function in our daily activities. We worry about things beyond our control. We let our problems overwhelm us. We need to relax and wait on God to work out our problems in his own time. When we wait and relax we get rest and strength.

I remember wanting to finish this book by a certain deadline. I wanted to get the final draft done within three months. I worked long hard hours. At first, the words came rushing out like a flood, filling page after page, then there came a time when the words were slower to come. I became discouraged and wondered if I would finish the project I believed God had given me to do. I laid aside my work for many months, wondering if I would ever get to the end. Concerned friends asked "How is the book coming?" My response was "Slow."

I had allowed self-doubt to come in and try to steal what God had given me to do. At times things did look doubtful.

There were times when I could not think of another word to write, so my project became dormant. It was not until God showed me people who could read what I had already written and could give me the positive feedback and the encouragement I needed to regain my self-belief. The Lord blessed me with people willing to help me make my dream come true. I rebuked self-doubt and reassured myself I was a winner and with God's help, I would finish my book, because I needed a job and God had given me a job to do.

So, when we are faced with an obstacle and we have done all we can do within our own strength to overcome it, we need to be still and see the salvation of God and get deeper in His Word. There are stories in there that will lift our spirits and help us fight off negative thoughts of gloom and depression.

The despondency of the prodigal son gives us examples of gloom and despair. When the prodigal son recklessly squandered his inheritance and found himself eating and sleeping with the pigs, he was in gloom and despair.

I believe when the prodigal son left his father's house with his share of his inheritance, he had prospects of finding more wealth. It is difficult for me to believe he imagined the day would come when he would have nothing. However, things didn't work out the way he planned. He realized his father's servants were better off than he was. When he felt he could no longer live with the pigs, he decided to return to his father's house to be with the servants. He had a hope for a brighter tomorrow.

The story goes on to tell us, when his father saw him coming from far off, dirty and barefoot, he was glad to see him. He had missed him. He sent for the best robe and shoes available and called for a feast to be held in his honor. He gave him a ring to be a constant reminder to him, of who he was, and to whom he belonged. A child of the King, a member of a RICH FAMILY.

We must realize we are children of the KING. We too have a rich inheritance. Our father is rich with houses and land, he holds all power in his hand. It is okay for us to want and have nice homes, automobiles and clothing. God wants the best for us so why should we settle for anything less? He wants us to be happy, free from worry or care, with peace of mind.

When we are at a point of hopelessness, and life seems dark and dreary, it is possible to lose focus on our hope and be lost for words. The best words, I know, that will turn a situation around are: Lord, Have Mercy. They are our battle cry for kindness and compassion and alleviation of distress.

Chapter 4
In Sickness

But he was wounded for our transgressions, he was bruised for our iniquities: the chastisement of our peace was upon him; and with his stripes we are healed. (Isaiah 53:5)

I never experienced any real illness or any concept of being sick until 1976. Sure, I had my bouts with common colds, headaches, and upset stomachs, but no real sickness. However, the company I worked for had a policy for each employee to have an annual physical and check-up.

That year, a routine x-ray showed markings on my lungs. The nurse received the report and informed me that it looked like Hodgkin's disease, a terminal cancer. The next few weeks turned into a nightmare. They scheduled me for further testing right away.

I can still remember the taste of that vanillin cream chalk-like milk shake they made me drink to do the liver scan. Today, I don't drink vanilla milk shakes. I had to lay on a table while the doctors took the tests. They put me in a tube, they turned me over and around, pressing here and there, probing here and there. I started to cry. They asked me if I was in pain, I replied, "No." I had no pain. I just didn't understand what was happening to me.

I had always been an active person. I didn't feel sick, look sick, or act sick. At that time, I was a recent divorcee, mother of a four-year-old daughter, a student at the University of Toledo majoring in business administration, and a full-time accounting assistant at Owens-Illinois, Inc. I attended church regularly, participated in church activities, sang in two choirs, was an active member of a gospel drama group and enjoyed living very much.

I was more afraid than anything. I had never heard of Hodgkin's disease before. I looked it up in a medical dictionary. The definition stated it had no cure and that most patients die within five years. Oh LORD! Have Mercy. Who wants to die? No one I knew and I certainly didn't.

The bottom line was I felt I was just too young to die. I was only 26 and had a lot of things I wanted to do. I wanted to finish school and see my daughter grow up. I simply wanted to live. Death seemed so final.

As with most individuals facing death, I went through several stages. First, I was angry with the nurse for telling me that I had terminal cancer. Who was she? What did she know, and why did she have to tell me I had terminal cancer? I didn't like her at all.

The tests I had taken as an out-patient did not reveal anything significant, so therefore the doctors decided to have me admitted right away for a biopsy of my lymph nodes and open chest surgery. Until that time, I didn't know I had any lymph nodes, only to find out I had eight. I was angry at everybody and everything. Why was this happening to me?

Friends and family members started to treat me differently. I could see the looks of bewilderment in their eyes, as they didn't know what to say or do. Some of them made me feel as if I was going to die right then and there. Co-workers wanted to know all the details, feeling sorry for me. I couldn't take the constant questions. "How are you feeling?" "What did the doctor say?" One of my closest girl friends called me up crying on the telephone, feeling sorry for me. I told her not to call me crying on the phone again. I am sure they all had good intentions. Even though I detested them feeling sorry for me, I went through the stage of feeling sorry for myself. It was a very difficult period in my life and often wondered, why me?

I didn't feel like eating, so I lost weight. I couldn't sleep at night, I began to look tired. I grew tired of the questions and became irritable. I almost accepted the fact I was going to die. The night before I went to the hospital, I could not sleep, I got up and started walking around my apartment. I walked from room to room talking to God. As I walked and talked, tears fell. I told God all about my fears and anxieties. I reminded him of the times when he had opened doors for me, and how he had watched over me and my daughter. I knew he made ways for me many times in my life. Then I simply told him. I did not want to die. I wanted to finish my college education and see my daughter grow up. I told him I was too young to die and I knew he had the power to heal me. I asked him to help me. I pleaded the blood of Jesus, fell on the floor crying, pleading the blood of Jesus. I reminded him that according to His Word, "But he was wounded for our transgressions, he was bruised for our iniquities: the chastisement of our peace was upon him; and with his stripes we are healed." (Isaiah 53:5) Those words had a personal meaning to me.

I thought of the woman who had an issue of blood for twelve years, who touched the hem of Jesus' garment and because of her belief was healed and made whole. I asked him for the same healing miracle.

As I laid on the floor crying, the LORD began to minister to me. He told me Jesus came so that I might have life and have it more abundantly. He did not guarantee a long life here on this earth. But, he did promise that by believing on him, I would have eternal life. He reminded me I was born to die and death could come at any time. No one knows the day or the hour when. As he dealt with my fears, he told me every day has potential for death, I could be in a car accident and die, be struck by lightning or die from a heart attack. He went on to list several ways in which I could suddenly and unexpectedly die.

He reassured me and told me not to worry. Regardless of what happened to me, my family would be there to take care of my daughter. As for my college education, it was only important that I finished as long as I had life. If I were to die, it would not make a difference if I finished college or not. In fact, I realized nothing would be important to me if I died. All of the people in my life and the things I wanted to accomplish were only important as long as I had life. I had no promises to live forever. Suddenly a peace came upon me. I decided to live until I die, to continue doing what I had been doing until I die. Go to school until I die. Raise my daughter until I die. Walk, talk, sing and serve God until I die.

Then I began to realize I had a lot to be thankful for. I started thanking God for everything he had done for me. Thanking him for protecting me and my daughter as I went to work and thanked him for protecting us as we slept at night. I started thanking him for everything I could think to thank him for.

I decided that if death was going to get me, it would just have to get me while I was doing what I had been doing all the time. I made up in my mind that death was going to have to catch me. I was not going to stop and let death take me. I would live until the day I died.

After my decision, I got up, dried my eyes, washed my face, went to my bed and said a little bedtime prayer my aunt taught me when I was little.

Now I lay me down to sleep,
I pray the Lord my soul to keep,
If I should die before I wake,
I pray the Lord
My soul to take.

I realized the true meaning of that little prayer!

The next morning I got up early, made the necessary arrangements for my ex-husband to take care of our daughter during my stay in the hospital. I washed and set my hair, gathered my makeup. Regardless of my situation, my appearance was still very important to me. Then I went shopping, bought a beautiful blue satin lounging pajama set and was packed and ready to go when my Pastor came to pick me up to take me to the hospital. Pastor Culp was somewhat stunned at my sense of calmness and peacefulness. He asked probing questions concerning the extent of my peacefulness. I told him

I was not worried, I had talked to God last night and he reassured me everything would be all right. Pastor Culp was a good pastor for me, he had taught me to trust and depend on our Lord and Savior Jesus Christ. As we rode to the hospital we shared times of prayer and thanksgiving to God for the wonderful things he had done for me. God had really blessed me. I was not worried about the operation. Truth of the matter, I never believed I would have an operation.

Everything went smoothly. The doctors and nurses were nice and friendly. The doctor who was scheduled to do my surgery was the same one who had operated on my stepfather the year before. He removed one of his lungs and my stepfather was doing fine. So I had confidence in the doctor.

Friends and relatives came to visit me the day before the operation. One friend came all the way from Washington, D.C. for moral support. I entertained my guest.

The morning of the biopsy, I woke up early, and made sure I looked my best, took a shower, combed my hair and put lotion on my face because I could not use makeup. My family and friends could not help but be in good spirits because I was in such a good frame of mind. When the orderly came to wheel me to the operating room, they followed behind us.

Once in the operating room, I recognized my doctor. They hooked me up to some machines, stuck a needle in my arm and asked me to count backward from 100. I did, but nothing unusual happened. I could still see, hear and talk. I remember the doctor and other people in the room talking. I couldn't understand why they were talking about the football game. I decided that since this was an important event for me, I would be the center of attraction. I began to talk, as my doctor was doing something to my neck. I told him he had operated on my stepfather and he was doing fine. I remember asking him if I could go home for the weekend. I wanted to go home because my boyfriend from Washington, D.C. had come to see me and I wanted to spend some time with him outside of the hospital. My doctor said if I felt like it, he would arrange for me to go home for the weekend because, the test results from the biopsy would not be ready until Monday. I could leave Saturday afternoon but I had to be back at the hospital Sunday afternoon. I felt that was a good deal. He finished removing the lymph node and I didn't remember anything else until I heard someone calling my name in the recovery room.

My poor mother, when the doctor told her I wanted to go home for the weekend, she looked at my friend and said she knew why, but felt I should stay in the hospital. As they were wheeling me to my room, my mother told me the doctor had told her I wanted to go home, but she thought I should stay in the hospital. I remember raising up off the bed and telling her the doctor said I could go home if I felt well enough to go. She realized how much I wanted to go home and allowed me to go.

I had missed my friend since he moved away. I wanted to spend some time with him. When he picked me up, we went to the park across the street from the hospital. He was sweet. At home he catered to me, fed me soup and watched over me while I slept. I was so tired I slept the whole time during my stay at home. The next day I was ready to go back to the hospital. When we returned to the hospital I had a high fever. The nurse gave me some aspirin which made me ill. My friend left and I fell asleep until a nurse woke me to confirm the open chest surgery scheduled for Tuesday. I told her I was not having open chest surgery and was extremely upset at the fact she asked me about one. The test results were not in from the biopsy and how dare she ask me about a surgery. I am sure she was only doing her job, but since I had claimed healing, the idea of a open chest surgery had been cancelled from my mind.

Monday morning, I got up early, showered, combed my hair and put on full makeup. I put on my pretty lounging gown and when my doctor came in I greeted him with a bright smile and said "Morning, Doctor, how are you today?" I guess my pleasantness and cheerfulness overpowered him. Every bone, muscle and substance in my body told him, I did not want to hear any bad news. He commented on my cheerfulness, and indicated that the test results were back and I did not have cancer, the biopsy of my lymph nodes was benign. There was no need for a chest operation and I could go home when I felt up to it, but to have another chest x-ray in six months and to give his regards to my stepfather.

Talking about one happy person, I thanked the Lord for what he had done for me. I called everyone I could think of to let them know the good news. I was not going to die. I was going to live. I made arrangements for my mother to pick me up the next day and went home to relax.

Throughout this ordeal, I lost weight, I was down to 100 pounds with all my clothes on. People were still afraid I was going to die and looked at me sympathetically. It took me a while to gain my weight back, and once I started gaining, it seemed as if I would never stop. I finally stabilized at 115 pounds and still have pictures of me looking like skin and bones. There are times now when I wish I had a little less fat and more skin and bones, but I can live with the little fat I have.

Of course, there were those who still believed I was going to die on the spot, who constantly reminded me I needed to have another x-ray taken. The nurse at work constantly inquired as to when I planned to have my next x-ray taken. My reply to her was "Since it's not bothering me, I was not going to bother it." I believed I was healed and did not want anyone to say anything to contradict my belief.

Finally, after a year had passed, I had another x-ray taken, the report of that x-ray showed the markings had diffused, markings were not as evident as previous reports. All tissues appeared to be normal. Well! I could have told them that. The Word of God is true. He was bruised for our iniquities and with his stripes we are healed.

The experience I had when I faced my proposed sickness may seem different that those facing actual sickness, but I believe the principle of healing is the same. I have heard stories of people who were healed miraculously of a known sickness based on their belief that God would heal them. God allowed his son, Jesus Christ, to come on earth to heal the sick, give sight to the blind and heal the brokenhearted. I have seen miracle healing of God's people not only in my life, but also in the lives of others.

One summer, my daughter broke her collarbone playing softball. I remember hearing stories about people breaking their collarbone and dying. Therefore, I was concerned, but I had faith in God and my daughter had faith in God for the healing of her collarbone. The doctors decided not to operate on her, not to put a pin in her collar to join the broken bones together, but to have her wear a cloth sling for six weeks. We saw the x-rays of the broken collarbone and it was broken pretty bad. We trusted the doctors and above all, we trusted God. The day we saw the final x-ray and heard the doctor proclaim, "It's healed" we knew God had worked his miracle of healing, and we thanked him for his tender mercies.

My Aunt Rose, who helped raise me from the time I was two-years-old to nine-years-old is a sweet lady. We always had fun. She took us to amusement parks and we did a lot of fun things. She looked after us as if we were her own. Recently, Aunt Rose suffered a stroke. She was 76 years old. She was paralyzed on her right side from her face to her feet. Her speech was slurred, she could not move her right arm, leg or any parts of her right side. When I went to see Aunt Rose in the hospital, I knew not to be sad, remembering my stay in the hospital and how much I detested someone feeling sorry for me. So, I decided to be cheerful regardless of her condition. When I entered, the room was full of sunshine. She was glad to see me. I talked to her like I always talked to her. She tried to tell me what had happened. I didn't understand what she was saying, but she was trying real hard. Her mouth would not cooperate with her tongue. Finally, she said something I could understand. She said, "LORD, HAVE MERCY." "LORD, HAVE MERCY, HAVE MERCY LORD." Those words were so plainly spoken, I repeated the words, and she nodded her head repeating the words, "LORD, HAVE MERCY."

One of my cousins had come with me, and after seeing Aunt Rose's condition he began to cry. It was hard for him to imagine Aunt Rose in this condition as Aunt Rose had been a mother to so many children of her sisters and brothers. Aunt Rose always had something good cooking in the oven, she always had a dollar to give and a joke to tell. Aunt Rose kept us laughing. She had given us encouragement along our life journeys when our parents were not around. I refused to allow him to bring me to tears, I kept smiling and talking. I tried to make Aunt Rose laugh. When she talked, I talked back, I did my best to understand what she was trying to say, and to hold a conversation with her. I reached within my self and tried to read her mind to understand what she was trying to tell me. She could understand me. She laughed at the funny things I said.

We knew Aunt Rose had strong faith in God, because she first taught us to believe and trust in God. She took us to church when we were young. I still remember the people crying and my not understanding why. Often times I would find myself crying too. Aunt Rose would talk to God. And I believed, if it was God's will, Aunt Rose would overcome her stroke and be well again.

I went to see Aunt Rose as often as I could. Although I lived in another city, I would take time off from work to visit her. The first hospital was only 45 minutes away, but then they transferred her to another hospital which was an hour and a half away. I would still visit her when I could, although the time between visits were longer than when she was closer. But each time I visited her she grew stronger, she was able to move her feet, raise her arm over her head, and talk better each time I came. I remember the first time I visited her at her new hospital. When I got off the elevator, I saw an elderly lady with gray hair sitting in a wheelchair with her head hanging down. At first I didn't recognize the lady to be Aunt Rose, because she had on a pink sweatshirt, sweatpants, and jogging shoes with white socks. I felt this could not be Aunt Rose, why would she be dressed for jogging? I looked hard at the lady, and much to my amazement, it was Aunt Rose. I smiled and called out, "Rosa, Rosa, is that you Aunt Rose?" She recognized her name and turned her head toward me and smiled.

That day I also had on a sweatshirt, sweatpants, and jogging shoes. When I teased her about being dressed for jogging, she laughed and motioned for me to wheel her into her room. We spent some good quality time laughing and talking. I combed and braided her hair. She enjoyed having me comb her hair. It had always been long and pretty. She kept a touch of light brown in her hair, but she had not had it tinted for a while and only the ends showed signs of color.

After I combed her hair, I sat in a chair next to her and shared a magazine with her, turning the pages slowly and reading her different articles. When it started to get dark, we both knew I had to leave because of my long trip home. She had instilled in me to be home before dark. I gave her a kiss, a hug and said goodbye.

When I left, I felt good all over. Not only had I the feeling of making her day, but somehow realizing she had made mine. Needless to say, Aunt Rose recovered from her stroke and at 77 years old is still going strong. I shall never forget her words in the time of her sickness. "OH LORD! HAVE MERCY."

Whatever sickness you are experiencing, cry out unto the Lord, ask him to have mercy on you. He will hear you and deliver you out of your distress. Let your sickness be an example of what God can do today. Some people read the Bible and read the stories of healing in the biblical days and feel "that happened then, at a different time and place with a different type of sickness, not like what I have, not what I am going through." Healing is for all of us. When we allow the miracle of healing to be manifested in our lives, we become witnesses of what God can do in times of sickness. We need only ask for mercy, believe and never doubt, and trust Him to heal us of our sickness.

Chapter 5
Motherless, Fatherless And Friendless

When my father and my mother forsake me, then the
LORD will take me up.   (Psalms 27:10)

We have no guarantees on life. We are the product of two individuals who gave us the opportunity to live. We had no promises that they will be with us until the end, or that they would stay together until we got on our feet. When we came into this world we came naked, screaming and crying, wanting comfort. Those around us comforted us. Nurses wrapped us in a blanket to give us a sense of security.

Our basic needs had to be met for our survival and mere existence. We needed food, shelter and clothing. But, we also needed to belong to someone, someone to *LOVE US* and someone to *TEACH US* how to survive in this world. That someone became known as our parents. It may have been just a mother, a father or a stranger. We needed someone. We would not have made it without the aid of someone.

Someone taught us how to eat, walk and talk. We became dependent and attached to them because they supplied our basic needs. Crying was the only thing we knew how to do. Later we learned to imitate their behaviors and learned how to laugh. We watched their display of emotions and learned them as well. We were sent to school to learn how to read, write and do arithmetic. As we learned, we began the process of becoming less dependent upon them. We became more dependent upon others, our school teachers, classmates, friends and other relatives. The dependence on others never stops. It is not expected to: we all *need someone to depend on.*

In *I ain't much, baby, But I'm all I've Got,* written by Jess Lair, Ph.D., Dr. Lair refers to a speech given by Reverend Carrol Ellertson, a missionary to the Zulus in South Africa.

31

"When you were born a Zulu, you were nursed at your mother's breast and carried on your mother's back with your bare skin against her warm, bare skin for two solid years. You were given more physical contact and more physical love and affection than probably any but a handful of children in American culture get . . ."

". . . When his two years were up and a new baby came along, it was time for him to be put down on the ground."

". . . When this little Zulu child cried because he needed to be carried and held, one of the older children picked him up and held him and carried him around. The child did not have just a mamma, but it also had a bunch of mamoos, who were all of the mother's sisters and other women who loved this child because they had been loved as kids."

Many babies are born to happily married couples in the United States, couples who nurtured them through their formative years, providing the maternal care and affection so vital to their existence. Parents who were able to participate in the process of developing and shaping young lives into healthy nurturing caring adults.

However, such is not the case for all babies. Some are separated from their parents at an early age, through death and divorces. With the divorce rate in the United States at fifty percent, there is a fifty percent chance that a child will be raised by one parent. Some will not be raised by their parents at all, but by other family members or strangers.

My parents had four children and separated when I was nine months old. My father took the four of us to Virginia, and in the divorce settlement, the four of us were divided into two groups. My older sister and brother were given to the custody of my mother, and the two younger children were given to my father. My brother was less than two and I was nine months old.

My parents were young when they married and faced many financial hardships trying to survive on wages earned as domestic workers and laborers. I love both my parents very much. I had a difficult time understanding what happened to our family. However, reading the Word of God helped me to understand. "When I was a child, I spake as a child, I understood as a child, I thought as a child: but when I became a man, I put away childish things." (1 Corinthians 13:11)

As I examined the lives of my parents, I had a better understanding of what happened to us.

My father had good intentions when he took us to live with him in Virginia. Although he struggled for mere existence, he loved his children. However, he enjoyed drinking with his friends and having a good time. The drinking would get out of hand and cause problems. He became aggressive, abusive and did or said things he later regretted. Although my father was always nice and loving to me, there were times when his actions were not acceptable to others. From time to time, we lived with different families, and when my father had a falling out with them, we had to find another place to stay.

This went on for several years during my formative years until he took us to live with our aunt in Baltimore. She had one child, a daughter who lived in Virginia. Although she did not raise her own daughter, she treated us as if we were her own.

She allowed us to play outside until it got dark. But told us to come in when it started to get dark outside. We were taught to be "street smart." We had fun. We skated on makeshift skateboards, rode double in the streets on other kid's bicycles.

We climbed and swung from trees on a tire and a rope. Someone threw the tire up to us, we would reach out and grab it and swing to the other side. No one ever fell, no one was scared. The only time I got into trouble for swinging from the tree was when my mother sent me a new pair of pants and I ripped a hole in the hip pocket. I got a whipping for tearing my pants but not for swinging from the tree.

We had fun doing anything, whether playing hide and seek, hopscotch or chasing lightning bugs, grasshoppers, ladybugs or frogs, we had fun. We were safe because everyone looked out for each other. Adults kept us in order and taught us to respect elders.

Although, my father did not live with us, he lived close by and visited us regularly. One day he told us he was moving to New York, but we had to stay with our aunt. I don't remember if he told us when he would be back. However, I did remember hearing him say he had to move because he could not find work. I don't remember how I made the adjustment. I loved him a lot and knew he loved me.

He would let me be with him when he and his friends drank beer at the bottom of Television Hill. They parked the car and listened to music, while I entertained them by pretending to be a singer, singing along with the radio. I could sing "Frankie and Johnnie" word for word with feelings and expression, as if I lived the song. Each time a song came on the radio, I would sing my little heart out. One night my father said to me "Girl, you keep singing like that, one day you will be on Television Hill!" I remembered those words always and often wondered if I would ever sing on "Television Hill." When my father left for New York, we missed him, but somehow we made the adjustment.

My brother and I had each other, but when my brother was playing with his friends and I had no one to play with, I would go to the cemetery across the street. There, I read the names on the headstones and picked flowers off the graves to take home to Aunt Rose. I chased and caught pretty butterflies and put them in my jar. We took old jars and put holes in the top with a rusty nail and a rock. I would spend several hours in the graveyard, having fun in my own little world; carefree, enjoying the sunshine and the beauty of the earth. No adult knew for sure where I was, but knew I would be home before dark.

I was seven years old and felt life was full of fun and laughter. My trips to the graveyard were fun for a long time until one day a fat grasshopper hopped under my dress and got caught between my dress and my slip. It scared me because I didn't know what it was. I pinched it and it squished. When

I pulled up my dress, I got scared at the size of the grasshopper. I knocked it off, ran out of the cemetery and never played there again.

In retrospect, I am thankful that God takes care of little children. There, I was alone but not showing loneliness, motherless, fatherless and friendless, but yet not alone. I found my comfort in the beauty of the earth, God's creations and the warmth of those gone home.

My mother has always been a beautiful, charming lady. She sent us pictures of herself, my sister, brother and her new husband and their son. She always remembered to send us something for our birthdays and special occasions. We got excited at the sight of a box wrapped in brown paper tied with a brown thick knotted string. We knew it was from our mother. She always sent us clothes and toys. The best present I ever received from her was a dancing doll. You could strap the doll to your hands and feet to dance with it. It was as tall as I was, and had red and white stripped legs. I don't remember if I ever told her how much that doll meant to me. He was my buddy.

Even though I was a baby when I last saw her, other family members kept her real for me. I missed her and longed to be with her.

Finally, one day we were informed that we would have to go and live with our mother, as Aunt Rose could no longer afford to keep us on her wages as a domestic worker. We were excited and could not wait until the day came when we would be with our mother. We were both excited and sad. We were excited to be reunited with our mother, but sad to leave our aunt who had loved and cared for us as if we were her own. It was a sad time for our aunt, because she loved us very much. However, we were so excited about our upcoming adventure and the prospect of seeing our mother, we didn't understand her feelings.

My brother was ten and I was nine years old when we left Baltimore to ride the "B & O" train to Ohio. Our aunt had given us money for food and two silver dollars for us to keep.

She made us promise to keep them and not to spend them, so we would never be broke.

We had fun on the train, hopping from coach to coach, running up and down the corridors, spending our monies for junk food, then begging food from strangers on the train. We slept, laughed and talked all the way to Ohio. By the time we arrived in Ohio, all of our money was gone except our silver dollars. We were hungry and a lady at the luncheon counter brought us cereal and milk.

As we anxiously waited for our mother to pick us up, we played a game of trying to guess who she was, since neither one of us had seen her since we were infants.

Each time a lady came into the station, we thought she was our mother. Finally, a man and three children came into the station. We studied them and figured the little boy to be about seven, the other boy 15, and the young girl about 20. We felt that they couldn't be for us because the girl looked too young.

But to our amazement, that young girl turned out to be our mother! She was happy to see us and called us by our names. We were surprised, shocked and stunned. We couldn't figure it out, she looked so young and pretty, how could she be our mother? She said she was, we accepted it and were glad to be reunited with her. The boys turned out to be our step-brother, our teenage brother and the man, our stepfather.

We were glad to be with our mother, but we had to make some adjustments. We were not allowed to play outside unsupervised. We could not climb trees or do a lot of things we were used to doing. Our life was structured. I was not allowed to play with the boys or play boy games. I couldn't rake the yard, cut the grass or do anything that was considered a boy's job.

However, I was taught to wash on a scrub board, hang clothes outside on the clothes line, iron, wash dishes, scrub and wax the floor on my hands and knees, dust furniture, get spider webs from the ceiling and do all sorts of general housekeeping.

This was all new to me. Occasionally, my aunt would let me help her with light housework, sweeping the floor or washing the dishes. The chores given to me by my mother were not fun. I hated housework. I had been used to running free in the fields, chasing butterflies. To be confined to the house doing housework robbed me of my free spirit.

My mother expected something different from me. She wanted to change me from being a "Tom Boy" and convert me into a lady. I rebelled. I felt trapped and wanted to escape to be the care-free person I had grown to be.

My mother was beautiful with long pretty hair, a real lady. Her fingernails were long and neatly polished. She wore red lipstick all the time and high heeled shoes when she was off work. She had a real nice shape and always looked nice in her clothes. I couldn't understand why she tried so hard to make me look like her.

My hair was always messy, my clothes would get dirty because I was careless and sloppy. I bit my fingernails, which drove her nuts. She did everything possible to get me to stop biting my nails. Nothing worked, but she never gave up.

It seemed to me she had made a vow to tame me. On the other hand, I had made a vow not to be broken. There were times when she must have felt she was trying to tame the shrew. We had our moments. There were times when I didn't like her and I am sure, she didn't like me either. In any event, we made it through. True enough, I ran away from home three times, and each time I was given the rod of correction and I am very grateful for her unfailing love and guidance.

One day, I looked in the mirror, and to my amazement, I saw myself neatly dressed with my hair in place, my lips brightened with red lipstick, my nails groomed and polished and standing tall in my high heeled shoes. Suddenly I realized, she had won and I was pleased. Now I have a teenage daughter and all I can say is: "Oh Lord! Have Mercy."

All of us experience times of loneliness without a mother, father or friend. But over the years, I have found a friend who has never left me. One who has stuck by me through sickness and health, good times and bad times. His name is Jesus. God's only begotten Son. He is always there when I need him. He has promised to comfort me when I am lonely, feed me when I am hungry and never to leave me alone. Knowing he is there gives me peace of mind. He can be a mother, father or friend we can depend on.

Chapter 6
Testing Love Through Emotions

There is no fear in love; but perfect love casteth out fear: because fear hath torment. He that feareth is not made perfect in love. (1 John 4:18)

The need for love is very strong, everyone needs to love and be loved. We have been conditioned to love and be loved. As discussed in the previous chapter, babies are taught to love and respond to expressions of love. Hugging, kissing and caressing become known as physical expressions of love. When we become adults we still have those needs.

When we don't get our love need met, we feel insecure, unstable, apprehensive and often lack self-confidence. Some of us can not think about anything else when we are suffering a love lost. In as much as love is such a strong force in our lives, the absence of it has its devastating aspects as well. Love is strong as death (Song of Solomon 8:6). And many waters can not quench love, neither can the floods drown it. (Song of Solomon 8:7).

Family members, friends and mere associates can not begin to fulfill our love needs. The need for love causes us to seek it from others. Oftentimes we become disappointed in the amount of love we receive from those we give love. This is the case in some male-female relationships whether it be a boyfriend-girlfriend relationship or a husband-wife relationship.

We are created to have companionship and relationship with members of the opposite sex. According to the Scriptures: And the LORD God said, it is not good that the man should be alone; I will make him an help meet for him. (Genesis 2:18)

When God created Adam, God gave Adam the opportunity to find a help mate, but none was found so God caused a deep sleep to fall upon Adam. While he slept, God took one of Adam's ribs, and made a woman who was made of his bones and flesh. The two were created to be as one. (Genesis 2:20-25) To be husband and wife. According to the Word of God it is the man's responsibility to search for the right wife (Proverbs 18:22) to love her (Colossians 3:19) and to be her leader. (Ephesians 5:23)

This is God's plan from the beginning of the creation of male and female. For this cause shall a man leave his father and mother, and cleave to his wife: and they twain shall be one flesh: so then they are no more twain, but one flesh. What therefore God hath joined together, let not man put asunder. (Mark 10:6-9) When God created Adam and Eve he created them to be compatible and capable of living together in a harmonious and congenial peaceful environment. To be companions, mates, a pair and a perfect match. He created them to be as one with each and as one in their faith in him.

Somehow, some of us have strayed from God's original plan for our lives. The men don't know who they want, and the women are leaders over the men, chasing them around, demanding attention. We find ourselves unequally yoked, but trying desperately to find some elements of love in devastating relationships in which we have placed ourselves. Even when the relationship causes us mental conflict and torment, we find ourselves constantly testing to see "if this is really love."

Impossible as it may seem, it is easy to find love, because love can be any strong feeling of affection or devoted attachment to a person of the opposite sex. We are even commanded by God to love everybody. For God is love.

However, we make our mistakes in relationships when we look for love rather than compatibility and companionship. When two incompatible people try to be as one, it becomes a test of opposites, which leads to discord, hostility, and anger. In some cases, the emotional state of the two turns into hatred if evidence of unfaithfulness, disloyalty and infidelity are allowed to creep into the relationship. Instead of existing in peace and harmony they become opponents, enemies and adversaries.

The emotional damage done by these relationships sometimes have long term effects.

Most of us have made our share of mistakes, when it comes to trying to find a mate. Some were fortunate enough to find their true mate the first time around. However, it is not so for a lot of us. Some of us are still waiting for our perfect mate to make us complete and be in order with the Will of God.

When we are in relationships outside the Will of God, we experience fear. There are many reasons for fear in trying to determine whether or not our affection is love. When we find ourselves getting involved in a relationship, we often wonder unconsciously if this person will be a good mate for us. Most of the time the answer is "no!" However, we try to make it work anyway but never totally committing ourselves because we are afraid to trust the other person. Oftentimes the reasons why we can not commit ourselves to others is because we KNOW that person is not for us. We know God does not want us screaming and hollering, fussing, cussing and fighting one another. Some of us try to make God responsible for our relationships by hiding under the acclamation "What therefore God hath joined together, let not man put asunder." (Matthew 19:5) If those conditions of misery and strife exist in our relationships, they are not of God.

Therefore, we should wait patiently for love and our mates. Because true love has no fears nor torment, but is kind, not easily provoked thereby bringing perfection and peace.

Chapter 7
Spiritually Blind

*One thing I know, that, whereas I was blind, now I
see.* (John 9:25)

Oftentimes we stumble through life merely existing from
day to day, month to month, year to year or living from
paycheck to paycheck not really accomplishing our life time
dreams, goals or aspirations. We often have meaningful
thoughts but never take action to make them become real.
Sometimes we wonder how is it that others get the breaks in
life and we don't. Sometimes we feel others have more of a
competitive edge than we do, or feel others must have had some
financial backing to get to where they are today. It is easy to
understand these feelings, as we live in a capitalistic society
where often times it is said "it takes money to make money."

In some cases, others have had financial backing or even
a competitive edge. Some had the good fortune to reap the
benefits of the labor of others, thereby making it easier to support and obtain their dreams, goals and aspirations. However,
not all of us have been financially blessed from the beginning.
Most of us are ordinary people with ordinary backgrounds,
nothing special which would seemingly make us stand out from
the rest of them.

Often, we become complacent where we are because we
can't see ourselves any other way. We can't see how to become the person we feel we were meant to be. A common expression states: "we can't see the forest for the trees." Our
minds become so preoccupied with the problems of today that
we lose sight of tomorrow. We walk around with invisible
shields on our eyes only seeing what is directly in front of us:
our immediate problem or concern.

I have found, as have thousands of others, we can have our blinders removed and see solutions to our problems as we read, study and meditate on the Word of God. When we cannot see a way out of our situation, he will reveal it to us if we seek it from him. When we allow him to show us his plan for our lives, he will give us a vision, a dream, a map, a plan or directions to get us to where we want to go. We need only to open our spiritual eyes to see.

We all have heard or read success stories of others, but as we examine those stories we can find several common factors in their success: a vision, faith in themselves, faith in others, action and perseverance. Where there is no vision, the people perish. (Proverb 29:18)

We must make the vision come alive. We all are capable of having visions and dreams. Daily we daydream on our jobs, using our imaginations to improve our work and surroundings. As we see the lives of others become prosperous, they inspire us. We admire their ambitions as they strive to achieve the finer things in life. We call them enterprising, powerful, creative, imaginative, aggressive and go-getters. We secretly wish we could be like them.

The difference lies greatly in their eagerness, willingness, effort and desire to achieve their goal: making a dream a reality.

Years ago, a couple friends suggested that I should write a book. Basically, they were referring to some of the trials and tribulations I had experienced in my life. The outcome of those experiences seemed noteworthy to them, thereby leading them to believe I should share them with others. The concept of me actually writing a book was so far from my perception, it became a standing joke when talking with my friends. Usually the triumph of the battles were direct results of my belief in God, where I had no choice but to ask for God's intervention for the solution. My strongest statement was "Lord, Have Mercy."

I thought the possibility of my writing a book was out of reach and therefore took no immediate effort to cultivate the possibility. Although in college I took several writing and communication courses as a requirement. In order to get a decent grade out of my courses, I wrote what I felt the instructors wanted to see or hear, not always what I wanted to say. However, they seemed pleased with my work. Although, I didn't feel it was of any great effort, I just did what I had to do to complete the class requirements.

Once I wrote an interesting story about an orange and called it "Mr. O & I." I wrote the story as if the orange was alive and gave it character. The instructor loved it. Years later I lost my copy, contacted the instructor to see if he still had a copy of the story. Sure enough he remembered the story and still had a copy.

I also experimented with poetry writing and purchased the *1976 Writer's Market* published by Writer's Digest. At that time, I had given some thought to trying to write short stories or poems professionally, although it never materialized. I wrote poems of inspiration and hope and gave them away as gifts. I did not submit one item for consideration to the publishers. I felt I would be rejected and not successful, so I didn't try.

I buried the dream because I had no vision or belief in myself. As I worked in various capacities in the business world, there were many occasions when writing was part of my job. I found myself writing office memos, procedural manuals, technical reports and even letters for other people's signatures. Changing my work was my greatest pet peeve. I could not understand how I would be asked to write a letter for someone else only to have their name signed to the final draft. After spending a considerable amount of time and effort on a draft, the signer would change a word by using a synonym. I had problems understanding if they couldn't come up with the ideas for the body of the text, why change the work by using a word that meant the same thing? The underlying problem was my need to have my work appreciated and accepted under my own name.

The last time the notion of writing a book came to me, the vision of the reality of it was so plain and simple, I had no choice but to try. By this time, I had read so many positive thinking books, they were all beginning to sound alike. Each time I would be in search for something new and different. Although the characters changed, each book was written by people who at one point in their lives were ordinary people. Some had earlier problems with self-esteem, and self-worth, but managed to overcome their obstacles and decided to share them with others. Many of them told of their personal relationship with God and what happened when they trusted and put their faith in him. I realized what he had done for them, he could also do for me.

It also made me realize the belief they had in themselves had not always been cultivated from a healthy family life. It does make life easier when we have someone to believe in us, but sometimes it takes time to find the right person who will believe in you or take you seriously. It is critical that we believe in ourselves, put our faith in God because he has faith in us.

All of us at one time or another have felt no one really believed in us or what we wanted to accomplish out of life. I have felt that way myself from time to time, but there were always a few faithful friends, who regardless of the project, had faith I would accomplish the task at hand. When I would lose faith, they kept my vision and hope alive.

Joan Smith is a personal friend of mine who suffers with glaucoma, a disease of the eye which caused her to lose some of her sight. Although she has undergone operations to save her remaining sight, her vision loss is permanent. As I shared with Joan my dreams and visions, they became real to her too. She could see where it was possible for me to attain my goals. Together we mapped out methods step-by-step to make them happen. We saw a lot together with our spiritual eyes. Her insights and perceptions on life took me beyond my own imagination. As her physical sight diminished, God blessed her, and increased her spiritual sight.

Successful people had periods in their lives when it was difficult to sell their ideas or talents to others. Sometimes others had difficulties believing in inventors or creators because of their limited vision of not being able to see the overall ramifications of the project.

There are writers, artists, musicians and designers who have become famous after their death. In spite of their seemingly fruitless efforts, they continued to believe in themselves and continued to work on their projects. Although they did not receive full recognition during their lifetime, they worked diligently believing that someday somewhere someone would believe in them.

When I started working on my book project, a lot of preliminary work needed to be done. I needed a publisher, a printer, an artist, a typesetter, an editor and an advisor just to name a few. In order to accomplish the goals I set for myself, other people used their skills and creativities to help make my job of writing easier. When we believe others have something of value and appreciate their efforts and they will in turn believe in us.

If you feel you have been inspired to create a product, sing a song, write a book, or start a business. Believe you can do it. If you seriously believe you can do it, you can make it happen for you. Don't let the lack of finance keep you from exploring the "What if's" in your life. Don't spend the rest of your life wondering what would have happened if you could have done this or that. None of us knows what tomorrow will bring. It has been said it could be sunshine or it could be rain. But when we allow God to open our eyes to see what he has in store for us, our blinders will be removed and we will be given visions not seen before: solutions to our problems and ideas for new projects. We will be able to see clearly, even though we were once blind to those visions, he will open our eyes to see.

Chapter 8
Misunderstood

Let my cry come near before thee, O LORD: give me understanding according to thy word. (Psalms 119:169)

All of us have been misunderstood at some point in our lives. Our speech misconstrued, our silence misconceived, our action misjudged and our reaction mistaken. Even our presence, interpretation or observations misunderstood. No matter what we said or did, we were misunderstood. When we are misunderstood, we feel confused and perplexed.

We have searched for understanding somewhere, and as the songwriter tells us, "not finding it anywhere." We all need understanding. Someone to share our secrets, successes, failures, dreams and aspirations. Someone we can relate to and who will empathize with us. Above all, we need someone who will comprehend and not take us for granted.

In as much as we want and need understanding, oftentimes we don't understand ourselves. How can we expect others to understand us, if we don't understand ourselves? Why do we say or do the things we do? The answers to these questions are buried deep within us. We need to get to the root of our action and reactions. Why do we make negative statements when we really mean positive ones? Often we find ourselves apologizing for our statements: "I really didn't mean it that way," or "I'm sorry, I thought you knew I was just joking," or "I didn't know it was going to hurt your feelings." Some of us try to cover up our own insensitivities by trying to make others feel guilty.

Before we can attempt to find out why others misunderstand us, we need to understand ourselves. What makes us tick? Sometimes, 30 to 40 years go by before we receive healing of the scars and wounds we received as children. Our understanding of ourselves as an adult is different than our understanding of ourselves when we were children.

When I was a child, I never gave thought to why my parents separated or what effect it would have on me as an adult. I accepted it as a part of life. It was not until later in life I searched for some answers as to understand why it happened. Painful experiences in trying to establish healthy relationships, forced me to wonder, why? I wondered why mainly to see if there was a pattern which affected my inability to establish a healthy stable relationship.

Through the help of friends, we examined my past to determine what effect it had on my present. The purpose of examining my past was to find where the problems first took form. When we look at history, we can plan for the future. Although we can not predict the future, we can use the past patterns of events as an aid in preparing for tomorrow.

As we analyzed my present state, we could understand some reasons for my failed attempts in relationships. We found my jealousies and insecurities were due to my lack of self-confidence and self-esteem. I had placed too much emphases on having the other person mean everything to me. My love became the smothering kind of love. I had the choking kind of love. I needed that person to do everything with me and be with me all the time. I wanted their activities centered around my needs and wants, not allowing them to have other friends or activities which did not include me. When things would not go my way, I would have tantrums and cry and later be embarrassed at my behavior. My demands were great and therefore I received little.

Some of the scars I received as a child had not healed. I still carried the fear of abandonment. I had been separated from my mother when I was nine months old, separated from my sister and brother before I was two, and left by my father before I was eight. And as a result, I lacked security within myself and needed to find it in someone else. I needed someone who would always be there for me, someone who would never leave.

My brother was the only person who was always there for me. We made a good brother-sister team. We were rough and tough. He fought the boys and I fought the girls. Children of the families where we lived became our extended family. Six boys and girls slept in the same room. We experimented with sex. Although we knew we were not supposed to do the things we did, we did them because they were fun. Sex was a game. We had no knowledge of its overall ramifications or what effect it would have on us as adults. We had no way of knowing that our sexual behaviors could be used against us in the way we feel about ourselves or others.

In examining the past of my parents, I realized a 15-year-old girl married a 21-year-old man. They had four children by the time my mother was 23. My father was a manual laborer, who stuggled to meet the needs of a family of six. He had only a third-grade education. I could understand him being stressed, over-burdened and feeling a need for a drink.

Life had not been a bed of roses for either of them. When they separated, they had little for themselves and even less to give to their children. My mother remarried, had another child, reclaimed her other children, continued her education, and has been happily married for almost 40 years. My father remarried, had another child, his second wife left him and he spent most of his life suffering the loss of his first family. He feels his greatest achievement in life is being the father of five children who have turned out all right.

The efforts we make in trying to understand others will depend on the closeness of the relationship and our willingness to look beyond their faults and see their needs. When we only look at the outward appearances, we cannot see the scars and wounds lying deep within the heart. But as we turn our lives over to God, he can look into our hearts and allow us to see ourselves and others as we really are, wanting and needing to be loved.

God is GOOD and God is GRACE and His MERCIES endure forever. Where there is shame and guilt, he replaces with goodness and mercy. Where there is confusion and strife he replaces with understanding, tranquility and peace.

When we feel misunderstood and want to know the reason why, we need to dig deep within ourselves and study ourselves awhile. Some questions will have answers and some will not. None of us will find all the answers. We must accept the fact that none of us is perfect and all of us have sinned and fall short when measuring up to God. But, when we go to him in prayer, he is faithful and just, to forgive us for our sins and cleanse us from all unrighteousness. And his peace, which we will not understand, will keep us until we reach the Promised Land.

As we go through misunderstanding, confusion and strife, and we have done our best to understand, we can be at peace with ourselves. Because we have a consolation of realizing that what we don't understand now, we will understand it better by and by.

Chapter 9
Making Your Best Good Enough

*I can do all things through Christ which strength-
eneth me.*   (Philippians 4:13)

Sometimes we become so caught up in our problems and
situations, we don't know what to do next. So many things
are going wrong and we find ourselves not knowing what to
do to make things right. The best place to start is where you
are. It takes only one step to begin a new project and beginning where you are is the only place to start.

When we need new jobs, we need to examine our current
skills and look for positions that pay for the kind of skills we
already have. When we need to make extra money, our spiritual
gifts and talents may be used to obtain what we need. Finding
out what abilities we already have is a good starting place to
achieve greater things.

I read a story about a widow with two sons, who was so
far in debt, her creditors were ready to take her sons to be
bondsmen to serve the creditor without wages.

The widow was worried because she had no visible means
of repaying the money she owed. She sought advice from
Elijah, a man she believed to be God fearing, and explained
to him she had nothing of value in her house to sell to gener-
ate the kind of money she needed to repay her debt. The only
thing she had that could be worth something was a pot of oil.

After listening to her situation, Elijah came up with an idea
to help solve her money problems. He told her to borrow a
lot of full and empty bottles from all of her neighbors. Then
after obtaining the bottles, to take her sons home, shut the
door and pour oil into all the bottles.

She took his advice and found out she had more oil than
she could find bottles to fill. Then she went back to Elijah for

more instructions. This time he told her to sell the oil, and pay her debt and indicated that she would have enough money left over for her family to live on. (2 Kings 4:1-6)

When I read the story, I wondered how many of us would still have all of our children if someone could take them away because we owed money?

In this story, the widower knew she was in trouble, her sons were about to be taken as collateral to be bondsmen. She sought help, took advice, acted in faith, believed and trusted in Elijah the man of God.

What was in the bottle of oil the widow filled behind closed door? Could it have been the beginning of "Trade Secrets"? Or could it have been a simple example of supply and demand? Once she had received all of the bottles from her neighbors, she added value to the bottle by filling them. Thereby giving her something to sell. What she put in the bottles we will never know. She had nothing except a pot of oil. She knew her oil was worth something but had no idea how to make it work for her. She needed guidance and directions.

The story of the woman with the pot of oil happened before the birth of Jesus Christ. But, when Jesus started his ministry, he performed miracles to non-believers so they could see evidence of what could happen in seemingly impossible situations if they would only believe.

I recently read an article in INC. Magazine, about a retired couple in Hawaii who had been in the baking business for nearly half a century. They lost almost all their retirement money in a money-making scheme. Can you imagine the disappointments faced by this couple? When they felt they had built a nest egg for their retirement years, only to lose almost everything to a thief who convinced them to trust him and give him their money. After the shock of the realization of having lost everything they had saved, the couple fell back on a skill they already had; each other, a roof over their heads and good baking skills. They had to re-group. They started baking pies in their own kitchen. Then they started selling them to others. The couple excercised "The Magic of Thinking Big," and decided to explore the possibility of exporting their product. This couple, according to the article, now have a $3 million-a-year pie business.

When we examine what we already have, we can find tools and skills already at hand that can be used to get us what we need. Our skills, knowledge and talents may be used by someone who will be willing to pay us for them. Read how others became successful doing your particular skill. If it can happen for them, it can happen for you. Whatever you have, use it. Think big of it, try it, test it, have fun with it and make the most of it. Success, fulfillment and prosperity is something we are entitled to.

We need to surround ourselves with positive thinking people and avoid negative thinking people, people who are always down. They will try to destroy our dreams, hopes, and aspirations. They can drain us emotionally. Don't let them get too close to you, but let them watch your progress from a distance, your positive energies will become strong and contagious, they will want some of your energy.

Encourage them to read the Word of God and other inspirational books written by authors who were inspired by God. They are designed to help us grow spiritually and mentally. They inspire and stimulate our intellect to help us unleash the creative energy within us.

Norman Vincent Peale was one of the first to write on the concept of positive thinking. *The Power of Positive Thinking* by Mr. Peale was published back in the fifties. His book has inspired others to lead successful lives using the POWER of Positive Thinking. The material in his book sinks into your soul and becomes a part of your life. Some of us use the material, others bury it. His teaching of the unleashing of the POWER of Positive Thinking has also inspired others to write similar books to reach people of various backgrounds and status in life.

Dr. Robert H. Schuller's book *Moving Ahead with Possibility Thinking* challenges us to change our thinking and our lives by positive thinking. Another one of his books, *Tough*

Times Never Last, But Tough People Do! tells us not to surrender to defeat, fear, frustrations or faults but suggests we affirm our abilities, have faith, commit ourselves, and make our dreams happen.

In the book, *The Magic of Thinking Big,* by David J. Schwartz, Mr. Schwartz discusses a unique way to magnify your thinking patterns to achieve the things we want: higher income, financial security, prestigious jobs, power and influence for greater enjoyment. He presents a planned program for living on a big scale in one's job, marriage, family life, and in social and cultural activities.

He indicates you need not have great intellect or great talent to be a giant among men, but need the habit of thinking and acting in the manner that brings success. I have found his work very inspiring and consider his book a must read for those wanting to reach their full potentials.

Thinking small will not help us out of our situation. When we are hungry and ask for food, it will only satisfy our hunger for the moment. But if when we are hungry and ask for a job, we plan to satisfy our hunger tomorrow. We don't need to just catch up on our mortgages or bills, we need to be able to pay them on time, on a regular basis.

In *The Secret of Getting What You Want by Knowing How to Ask for the Moon and Get It,* by millionaire Percy Ross, Mr. Ross shows us how to master the most powerful and neglected secret of success: knowing how to ask for what we want. Mr. Ross' philosophy is based on the biblical scriptures: You have not because you ask not, ask, and you shall receive.

We should not be afraid to dream. I have read countless stories of people who had recurring dreams of doing something or becoming someone great that seemed impossible to others, but because they refused to let anyone take their dream away, they kept dreaming and believing their dreams would someday come true. Some had their dreams manifested well beyond what their own minds could imagine. So keep dreaming and imagining the "what ifs," because without dreams and visions we have nothing.

Talking and thinking about our dreams will not make them happen, we must do something about them. When we make an attempt or take a risk we venture into the realm of possibility.

I become irritated when I hear someone say, "I could have gone to college but my parents didn't have the money to send me," or "I could have gone in business, but I didn't have the money," or "I could have done this or I could have done that but something came up." I strongly believe, if there is something you want to do, you should at least try and see if you can make it come true.

There are people who have either lost an arm or leg, or their sight or hearing and have become successful enterprising individuals, making the best with what they have left.

All of us have some kind of handicap whether visible or invisible. Readily we can understand the visible handicap, but the invisible handicap is any area in which we fall short. It is good to know your invisible handicap and limitations because it gives room to work with what you have left, thereby allowing you to make all of your good attributes work for you Even the Army invites us to "Be All That You Can Be." If you have tried and failed in your attempts, at least you tried.

Making deadlines for yourself will help in attaining short-term and long-term goals. A commitment to work on what we want to accomplish is the beginning of the process to attain our goals. It all begins with what are we going to do today and tomorrow. When our plans are made, we must try to stick to them.

In writing this book, I found myself in debt and not really wanting to work for anyone else. The only thing I felt I had was time. I examined myself, sorted out what I could do and took an inventory of what I had. I realized I did have a lot of abilities. One of them was writing. I wondered if I had the gift to write. Then I realized I liked to write. Over the years, many of my friends have said, "Shirley, you should write a book." So, I considered the possibility. I have read many inspirational books which I felt I could have written. I had a a personal computer, a nearby library, plenty of paper, therefore, I made a decision to write a book.

I was not sure about the contents of the book, but after much prayer and meditation, I received guidance and directions from the LORD and acted upon them. First we mapped out our marketing strategies. The Who, What, How and When. Who would be the readers? What would I write? How would I market it? And when would I finish it?

We made our plans and set our goals, which made us set and meet deadlines. Sometimes we did not meet all of our deadlines. There were some trials and tribulations along the way, but through the grace of God and perseverance we made it.

It is important to set goals, because goal-setting gives you something to reach toward. Attacking and achieving a series of smaller goals cuts the seemingly impossible task into attainable little pieces, allowing you to take one step at a time until you reach your ultimate goal.

Once we set our goals and make plans and methods of achieving them, we must execute them. We must make every possible effort to bring them to pass, therefore making them become realities. Make something exist from a non-existent state.

Goals and plans can be obtained through the exercise of faith. The Word of God tells us that "faith is the substance of things hoped for, the evidence of things not seen." (Hebrews 11:1) There is no substance or evidence of what we hope for, but we must have faith to believe that it will be. For we walk by faith and not by sight. (2 Corinthians 5:7) We must first believe that all things are possible and put our faith into action.

When we drive to the store, we seldom wonder if the car will make it (unless it is like my old Chevy). But if the car is in good stable running condition, we don't worry about it making it to the store. We excercise faith in our cars and believe it will take us to our destinations. When we have faith in God, he will take us to where we want to go.

What good is it for us to have faith that will move mountains, if we don't exercise our faith and put it into action? We need to have faith in God, have faith in our projects, believe in ourselves, and put our faith into action.

When we believe in ourselves, we can get others to believe in us. The song "If you Believe," written by Charlie Smalls for the Broadway musical "The Wiz," is a story of a good person telling a lost child to believe in herself deep within her heart, to realize that no matter how others might try, no one had the ability to change the path in life in which she had to travel. She was told to trust her own true feelings and by believing, she would have enough courage not only to get her by, but enough to last her whole life. Her courage would be enough to make things happen. Then finally, she was told, if she believed in herself strongly enough, others would believe in her and she could also believe in others.

This song has meaning for all of us. Although Dorothy wanted to believe in a good witch, we must believe in God, ourselves and then our fellow man.

In our efforts to get to where we want to go, sometimes we will fail in our attempts. Most of us have heard the statement "Quitters never win and Winners never quit." It will be necessary sometimes to quit or let go of something we have tried. Sometimes when we try to force a situation we only make it worse and run into stumbling blocks rather than solutions. Rather than leaving the problem alone, we continue to work with it fruitlessly until we have made a complete mess.

There is a time to let go and try something new. Think of all the people who quit their jobs only to find better ones. All our past Presidents did not start out being President of the United States. One we know used to be an actor. Most corporate owners worked for someone else before starting their own companies. Therefore, there will be times when you must quit, let go and try something new, but keep trying. "To everything there is a season, and a time to every purpose under the heavens. A time to be born, and a time to die; a time to plant, and a time to pluck up that which is planted; a time to kill, and a time to heal; a time to break down, and a time to build up; a time to weep, and a time to laugh; a time to mourn, and a time to dance; a time to cast away stones, and a time to gather stones together; a time to embrace, and a time to refrain from embracing; a time to get, and a time to lose; a time to keep, and a time to cast away; a time to rend, and a time to sew; a time to keep silence, and a time to speak; a time to love, and a time to hate; a time of war, and a time of peace.'' (Ecclesiastes 3:1-8)

So we need not be discouraged when it is time to quit. Quitting may be the beginning of a new career, project or dream. We must, however, begin.

And when we begin to receive our blessings from the fruit of our labors, we need to share them with others. Not only our fruits, and talents, but also our stories. Our stories may be an inspiration to someone who is struggling to make their dream a reality. Our struggles and triumphs will become their source of encouragement as they strive to make their best good enough.

Chapter 10
Tears Of Joy

They that sow in tears shall reap in joy. (Psalms 126:5)

After we have experienced the tears of sorrow from our broken hearts, shattered dreams, lost love ones and countless other trials and tribulations in our lives, we can look to the hills from which comes our help and thank God for all that he has done for us. We can start by thanking him for the little things as well as the big ones. He did them for us because he loves us and wants what is best for us. He cares for us.

When we thank him for the things he has already done, we make room for more blessings to come. It would be great to have a life totally free from pain. However, the things which bring us joy also bring us pain. We will never know the wonderful feeling of joy if we never suffer pain. In most cases pain is somewhere lurking behind joy. Pain comes to steal our joy. God's power can ease our pain and allow us to regain our joy. Joy and pain go together like sunshine and rain with few shades of gray in between. A cloudy day comes from time to time. But for the most part, we have either sunshine or rain, good times or bad times, sickness or health thereby limiting the times when the two conditions simultaneously exist.

However, there were times when I was not content with my job because I had a recurring dream of becoming a movie star. The words of my father stayed in my mind "girl, you keep singing like that, one day you will be on Television Hill." The words were so strong that I had to at least try to make his dream come true. However, I had heard and read stories of actors and actresses who lived lives of poverty before becoming great movie stars with wealth and fortune. Somehow, deep in my conscious mind I had resolved myself to believe

61

that I had to suffer, pay my dues, starve, and give my all in order to become a movie star.

I quit a stable job as an accountant at Howard University to pursue my acting career. With no clear directions or outline as to how I should achieve my goal, I contacted a couple of local casting agencies. One of them turned me down completely and the other agency encouraged me to keep trying and keep believing in myself.

Although the second agency did not find me long-term work, the encouragement they gave me was valuable, which enabled me to go back to the first casting agency and be accepted.

My first jobs at the agency were liquor promotions, promoting wine coolers in liquor stores and cigarette promotions, passing out free cigarettes on street corners.

Somehow I believed by doing the jobs offered to me by the agency I would be paying my dues to become a movie star. Payment for those jobs were slow, sometimes I had to wait two or three months to receive payment. I would stay at home waiting for the telephone to ring, hoping for a call from the casting agency.

I spent money for pictures, acting lessons and union dues instead of buying food and clothing. I walked around looking like a bag lady with an old oversized brown coat, unsightly hat and worn-out boots and shoes.

My bills were not being paid. My landlord tried to take me to court for being late on my rent. My 13-year-old daughter did not understand what was happening to her mother.

There were times when I didn't know what to do, or how my rent or telephone bill would be paid. Times when I was not sure where my next meal was coming from. Although I had allowed myself to be in the situation, and the problems I experienced were of my own making, because of some mistakes I had made along the way. I have accepted my mistakes, by realizing that I am not perfect and do not make claims of being "Holier than Thou." But there is one thing I do know, God had compassion on me and helped me out of my distress.

He knew that as a professing Christian I should not have been out on the streets passing out cigarettes or in the liquor stores promoting wine or liquor, but he allowed me to do it for a reason.

One Sunday morning while ushering in my white uniform at my church, a little boy ran up to me excitedly patting me on my shoulder asking me "Aren't you the one who was selling the smoker cigarettes?" I was convicted by the Holy Spirit, I sheepishly nodded my head yes and quickly turned away. As I prayed that morning I asked God to forgive me for not displaying a positive image to that child.

God is good and merciful. He showed me a way in which I could star. I started working for my cousin in his business. The LORD blessed me to use the talents I had acquired in the business world to help my cousin. Blessings began to flow greater than my expectations. Those old clothes and shoes were replaced with new ones. My repossessed car was replaced with a new car. I started to think positive thoughts. My thoughts were put into action. We got results and the tears of joy filled my soul.

I have found that whatever state we are in, we can use it to be a turning point in our lives. When we read and meditate on the Word of God, he will guide and direct us to where we should be. When we allow his words to become real in our lives, he will show us a way out of our situations.

Even though things may seem to be tight, it does not mean it will remain that way forever. Things are constantly changing, people change and situations change. But the Word of God is true: Blessed are ye that weep now: for ye shall laugh (Luke 6:21) Weeping may endure for a night, but joy cometh in the morning (Psalms 30:5) and the comfort in knowing that: They that sow in tears shall reap in joy. (Psalms 126:5)

When we rejoice in the goodness of the Lord, and allow his peace which passes all understanding come into our lives, he will turn our tears of sorrow into tears of joy!

Things Remembered

It is not Aunt Rose's leaving that will hurt us the most.
For we are all here on borrowed time,
with no promises for tomorrow.
And in time, we too, must go.

But, it will be the things remembered that will make us sad.

Her times of caring, her times of laughter,
her times of sharing, her times of giving.
And, her time of living.

She was our mother, our sister, our aunt and our friend.

She gave to all of us.
And, it is so hard to say good-bye,
to someone from whom,
we have received so much.

But this we must,
because she is gone to a better place,
where there will be no more sickness and no more sorrow,
to take her rest and be at peace not worrying about tomorrow.

We can cherish her memories
and let her live in our hearts,
until we see her smiling face again,
when we too, must depart.

Shirley A. Fitzgerald
January 8, 1990